When Trauma Writes The Story Triumph Wins!
SHADOWS OF TRAUMA TO STREAMS OF GRACE

BOOK FIVE

Dr. Kayla Bullard

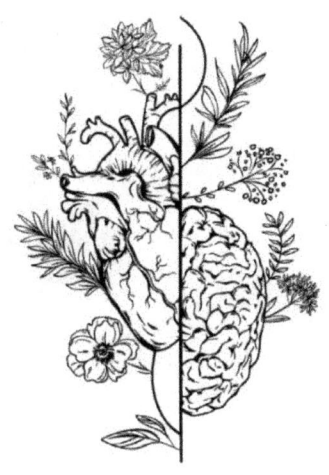

SHADOWS OF TRAUMA TO STREAMS OF GRACE

NO part of this book may be reproduced or transmitted in any form by any means, electronic or mechanical, including photocopying and recording, or by any information storage and retrieval system, except as may be expressly permitted in writing from the author. For more information, email drkaylabullard@gmail.com.

ISBN: 979-8-9927612-5-2

Published by:

www.owlpublishers.com

360 S Market St, San Jose, CA 95113, United States.
Printed in the United States of America

DEDICATION

To my new POE, Sister LaShika "Deer" Fonmanu,

Your very name, meaning "deer" in Japanese, speaks of sacred symbolism, gentleness, agility, grace, and divine attentiveness. You embody all of these with quiet strength and radiant resilience.

Like the deer that flees from the shadows into the safety of still waters, your life is a living testimony of hope rising from hardship, of grace emerging from grief. Your steps echo the rhythm of healing, and your presence brings calm in chaos.

You understand this sacred story not as an observer, but as one who has lived its truth, who has felt the ache of trauma and yet found the courage to run toward healing streams.

Your friendship is timely. Your heart, divine.

Your life is deeply treasured.

With love and honor, Dr. Kayla Bullard.

FORWARD

Endorsed & Scripted by Yahweh!

"מוסמך ומבושל על ידי יהוה!"

PREFACE

This book was born from a place of empathy
and deep spiritual reflection.

Psalms 42:1-2 (NIV) expresses the deep spiritual longing and thirst for God, drawing a beautiful analogy between a deer's longing for water and the soul's yearning for the presence of the Almighty.

In this poignant passage, this psalm deeply reflects on worship, praise, and deep spiritual meditation. In these verses, the image of a deer panting for streams of water vividly captures the intensity of the psalmist's longing for God, emphasizing the profound yearning for a connection with the living God.

"My soul thirsts for God, for the living God." This verse poses many questions and challenges believers to examine what they are truly thirsty for. Are we longing for God as desperately as we need water? Do we prioritize spending time with Him, drawing near in prayer, worship, and meditation on His Word?

The good news is that Jesus Himself affirmed this truth in John 7:37, saying, "Let anyone who is thirsty come to me and drink." God is not distant. He is ready to quench the thirst of those who seek Him sincerely. This verse calls us to recognize our need for Him and actively pursue a deeper, living relationship with the God who satisfies the soul. The desperate longing for water reflects the earnest psalmist's desire for communion with the Divine, expressing a longing that resonates with believers across time.

The imagery of the deer conveys not only a deep spiritual thirst but also an inherent trust that the water it seeks will be found.

In the same way, our souls must seek the presence of God with the assurance that He is near, ready to quench our deepest spiritual needs.

There are moments in life when the soul cries out, not with words, but with desperation. This is the story of such a cry. SHADOWS OF TRAUMA TO STREAMS OF GRACE is more than a tale of survival in the wild; it is a spiritual parable of what it means to be pursued by danger, overtaken by trauma, and ultimately rescued by divine love.

Euley, a young deer, represents the vulnerable places within each of us, the part that trembles when hunted by fear, grief, and loss. Her journey through the forest mirrors the emotional terrain many trauma survivors must navigate: the isolation, the flashbacks, the exhaustion, and the aching question, "Will I make it out alive?"

But Euley's story does not end in despair. As she runs, she finds something greater than escape; she finds restoration. Her cry is heard not only by creation, but by the Creator. And in the stillness of a hidden stream, she receives the healing that only heaven can provide.

Whether you are recovering from trauma, searching for peace, or longing to hear God's voice in the chaos of your own life, may this story be a gentle guide. Let it remind you that even when you are hunted by pain, you are never forsaken. You are seen. You are heard. And healing is possible.
Welcome to Euley's journey. May it awaken your own?

"As the deer pants for streams of water, so my soul pants for you, my God. My soul thirsts for God, for the living God." Psalm 42:1–2a (NIV)

Table of Content

INTRODUCTION 1

CHAPTER ONE 3

CHAPTER TWO 8

CHAPTER THREE 11

CHAPTER FOUR 18

CHAPTER FIVE 26

CHAPTER SIX 29

CHAPTER SEVEN 33

CHAPTER EIGHT 39

CHAPTER NINE 43

CHAPTER TEN 47

CHAPTER ELEVEN 50

CHAPTER TWELVE 59

CHAPTER THIRTEEN 62

CHAPTER FOURTEEN 65

EPILOGUE: THE ECHO AFTER THE CRY 71

REFLECTION 74

THE IMPACT OF SPIRITUAL HEALING AND PRAYER 78

A PRAYER OF RELEASE 81

A PRAYER OF HEALING 82

A PRAYER FOR FREEDOM FROM TRAUMA 84

A PRAYER FOR TRIUMPH FROM TRAUMA 86

INTRODUCTION

Psalms 42:1-2 (NIV) paints a tender and powerful image of spiritual yearning. It expresses the deep spiritual longing and thirst for God, drawing a beautiful analogy between a deer's longing for water and the soul's yearning for the presence of the Almighty:

"As the deer pants for streams of water,

so my soul pants for you, my God.

My soul thirsts for God, for the living God.

Where can I go and meet with God?"

This powerful passage is part of a larger psalm attributed to the sons of Korah, a distinguished group of Levites who served in the house of God. Entrusted with responsibilities in worship and music, they played a vital role in the spiritual life of both the tabernacle and the temple. The psalms credited to them are rich with themes of reverent worship, heartfelt praise, and profound spiritual introspection, offering timeless expressions of a soul's journey toward God.

In these verses, the image of a deer panting for streams of water, vividly captures the intensity of the psalmist's longing for God, emphasizing the profound yearning for a connection with the living God. The heartfelt question was posed in the last line: "Where can I go and meet with God?" This reveals an earnest cry of the heart of mankind for intimate fellowship with the Father. This longing was placed in man from the beginning of time. God's design was always for his children to know him and to walk with him in sweet communion.

The deer, though surrounded by hidden dangers in the forest, is guarded by an unseen presence, shielded from harm by a force far beyond its understanding. This powerful image inspired the story of Euley, a reflection of the unwavering protection found in God's love for His children.

Just as the forest seemed alive with divine defense, Scripture declares: "Whoever dwells in the shelter of the Most High will rest in the shadow of the Almighty. I will say of the Lord, 'He is my refuge and my fortress, my God, in whom I trust.' Surely, He will save you from the fowler's snare and from the deadly pestilence. He will cover you with His feathers, and under His wings you will find refuge; His faithfulness will be your shield and rampart." (Psalm 91:1–4)

This divine covering is not a poetic fantasy; it is a real promise available to every soul on earth. But it is accessed through a personal relationship with Jesus Christ. By receiving Him as Lord and Savior, we step into the shadow of the Almighty, under the shelter of His grace where love becomes our refuge and His protection, our hiding place.

CHAPTER ONE

Deep within a dense forest, where sunlight danced through the thick canopy above, a graceful deer named Euley wandered away from her herd, drawn by a spirit of curiosity and freedom. The air was rich with the scent of wild raspberries and with joyful anticipation, she followed the trail, eager to taste the sweet treasures hidden among the towering trees and lush undergrowth.

She remembered the spot well, an inviting patch she had discovered weeks earlier when her family first journeyed into their new home in the Westport Wildlife Sanctuary. Drawn by the memory and the promise of delight, Euley slipped quietly away from her herd. With each careful step deeper into the forest, she was guided not just by instinct, but by the yearning to satisfy the sweet craving that beckoned her forward.

Surrendering to the delight of her palate, Euley was lifted by the serenity and beauty that surrounded her. The peaceful stillness encouraged her to frolic freely, dancing across the open fields with carefree joy. Bathed in golden rays of sunlight, she moved absentmindedly, unaware that she was slowly drifting beyond the watchful eyes of her family.

Her sleek coat, a tapestry of chestnut and ivory, glistened beneath the filtered sunlight that streamed through the treetops. Each graceful movement revealed the strength and elegance woven into her slender frame. Patches of white traced her sides like delicate brushstrokes, blending seamlessly with the forest's natural palette.

Euley's eyes, gentle, wide, and the color of warm amber, held quiet wisdom and wonder, mirroring the stillness of the sanctuary around her. As she walked through the maze of foliage, her steps were measured and poised, a silent ballet of instinct and purpose. The tangled underbrush offered no resistance to her nimble stride; she moved as though the forest itself parted in reverence to her presence.

Euley felt a deep, sacred connection to the earth beneath her hooves and the whispering winds that carried echoes of ancient stories through the trees. Every rustle of leaves and chirp of birds became part of a living symphony, and she moved in harmony with it, pausing to graze on tender grasses and savor the sweetness of wild raspberries. As she bowed her head to feed, a quiet reverence settled over her. Her thoughts drifted to the Creator, whose presence she felt in every breeze and blade of grass.

Gratitude stirred in her heart as she remembered how her family had once been driven from their former home, fleeing the threats of human hunters and the wildfire that devoured the mountainside. Now, to have found such a haven, a forest untouched and full of peace, felt like a divine gift, an answered prayer from the Lord Most High who had not forgotten them.

Their new home was a breathtaking sanctuary, wrapped in comfort and beauty. Gentle hills rolled like velvet on either side, blanketed in a tapestry of wildflowers that painted the landscape with splashes of color. In the distance, a vivacious, chorus of wildlife brought the scene to fullness; squirrels darted playfully through the trees while Canaries and Blue Jays filled the air with their sweet, harmonious songs. Monarch butterflies, vibrant and whimsical, fluttered like sentient petals, waltzing gracefully through the air and weaving themselves into the lush greenery that surrounded them. It was a scene so rich with wonder that it felt like creation itself was rejoicing.

As Euley breathed in the crisp, fragrant air and savored the sweetness of the succulent fruit, her heart swelled with quiet joy. In that still moment, she lovingly embraced the presence of her Master, the One who formed her, who breathed life into her being. She cherished these moments of solitude when she could walk and talk with her Creator, the One responsible for her very existence. All around her, she felt His handiwork, the careful strokes of a divine Artist who painted every detail, from the tallest tree to the tiniest petal.

On this tranquil afternoon, Euley was enveloped in His presence, cradled in the splendor of a world lovingly spoken into existence. The soft brush of nettles grazed her hind legs as a gentle breeze whispered through the trees. Stretching her neck, she reached for a cluster of ruby-red wild berries, their sweetness bursting across her tongue. "Oh, how sweet and juicy!" she thought with delight. As she wandered along the winding, scenic paths, munching, marveling, and soaking in beauty, time slipped quietly away. Lost in the wonder of creation, Euley moved with peaceful abandonment, unaware of how far she had strayed.

Suddenly, the sharp crack of a gunshot pierced the air, shattering the forest's peaceful symphony and sending waves of panic through its inhabitants. Euley froze, her ears standing alert, every muscle tense with dread. In that instant, the stillness gave way to a primal instinct: run. Without hesitation, she launched into motion, her small frame cutting through the underbrush like a streak of wind. Her powerful legs pounded the forest floor as her heart thundered in her chest; each beat echoing the rhythm of survival.

Branches clawed at her sides, but she pressed on, breath ragged and shallow. Fear widened her eyes as adrenaline surged through her veins. Every leap, every bound became a desperate plea, "God, help me… deliver me."

It was more than instinct; it was supplication. "When the righteous cry for help, the Lord hears and delivers them out of all their troubles" (Psalm 34:17). And though she could not see it, heaven had already begun to move on her behalf. With danger on her heels and hope in her heart, Euley ran for her life; the forest now a blur around her fleeing form.

Racing through the forest, Euley's thoughts swirled in a storm of confusion, fear, and disbelief. Where had the shot come from? This was supposed to be a sanctuary, a sacred refuge where no hunting was allowed, a place of peace. Yet, danger had penetrated its borders. Her legs moved instinctively, but her mind struggled to make sense of the breach.

As panic threatened to consume her, a familiar scripture surfaced like a lifeline from within her soul: "Why, my soul, are you downcast?" (Psalm 42:5). Ancient words rose like a cry in the wind, pleading against the weight of fear. "Why so disturbed within me?"

In the middle of her frantic flight, something unexpected happened: a stillness, soft and steady, began to blanket her heart like a gentle rain. Amid the chaos, the echo of divine truth broke through. "Put your hope in God," she whispered through trembling breath, her voice nearly lost in the rustling trees. But the words anchored her, even as the shadows pressed in.

With renewed resolve burning in her chest, Euley surged forward, driven by the fierce will to survive. She tore through the dense foliage, leaping over rugged terrain, her limbs fueled by sheer determination. Each stride became a declaration of strength, a reflection of the unbreakable spirit within her.

Though fear still clawed at the edges of her mind, she clung to the hope of deliverance her soul aching for the peace she had once known.

"Deep calls to deep in the roar of your waterfalls... Psalms 42:7" The words echoed through her spirit, rising like a song from the depths of her being. They weren't just scripture; they were a cry, a lifeline. Guided by an invisible compass, Euley shifted her course midstream without hesitation. Her body responded to an inner whisper; the God of her soul was a divine GPS, pulling her toward refuge.

As shadows thickened behind her, she sang softly into the wind, a quiet anthem of defiance against despair. "All your waves and breakers have swept over me... Psalms 42:7" The storm had come, but she was still running, still believing, still holding on.

Fleeing with desperate urgency, Euley's once-fluid, elegant strides had transformed into erratic bursts of motion, frantic, disjointed, fueled not by freedom but by terror. Her breath came in short, ragged gasps as panic gripped every muscle in her body. The forest, once her sanctuary, now felt like a maze of threats closing in on all sides. Each pounding hoof beat echoed the thundering of her heart, carrying not just her body forward, but the weight of a trauma too great for words.

CHAPTER TWO

The sharp crack of the gunshot still rang in her ears; a sound she had heard too many times in the past, a cruel and violent punctuation that shattered silence and innocence. It was the same sound that had once sent her family fleeing through flames and smoke, dodging bullets and chaos as wildfires ravaged the mountainside. Though Westport Woodland Glades had promised safety, peace, and renewal, the illusion had crumbled in an instant.

The sound of the gun had awakened every buried memory, resurrecting the terror she thought she had left behind. The fear wasn't just of the bullet, but of what it represented, a world that could turn violent without warning, a world where even sanctuaries could be violated. And with every step, she wasn't just running from a hunter… she was running from the ghosts of all she had already endured.

The pounding of her hooves stirred not only the fallen leaves beneath her but the buried memories within her. Then, like a sudden gust of wind, the present dissolved.

In an instant, I was no longer running through the dense forest, fleeing for my life. I was back in the meadow with Gayle, back when the world was still soft, still kind. The morning had been calm, its breeze dancing over the open field, rustling the wildflowers and berry shrubs. Sunlight filtered through the canopy above, scattering golden patches across their backs as they foraged side by side. Our laughter mingled with the birdsong, and everything felt safe, whole.

Then, BANG!

The disturbance ripped through the silence like a storm

tearing through a dream. I froze. My mind couldn't make sense of it. The sound was too sharp, too violent, and too wrong for a place that had always felt like home. Time slowed. I turned just in time to see Gayle's eyes widen, filled with confusion and fear. Her body jerked once, then crumpled. Her legs gave way like broken twigs beneath her, folding awkwardly as she collapsed into the grass.

Then I saw the blood. It spread too fast; the deep crimson spread across Gayle's flank, staining her soft fur and pooling into the earth like spilled wine. The blood spilled onto my hoofs like a tattoo. The green of the meadow, once vibrant and alive, now stood in eerie contrast to the dark red that oozed between my trembling hooves. My heart stopped. My breath caught. "Gayle?" The name escaped my lips in a breathless whisper, barely audible. But I didn't move. My chest tightened. I was rooted in place, paralyzed by the horror unraveling before my eyes. Gayle's chest heaved once… then again… "Run…" came the faintest whisper from Gayle's lips, her final plea hanging in the air. And then, stillness. Nothing!

The wind died. The forest seemed to hold its breath. I took a single, staggering step toward my fallen friend, while the metallic scent of her blood hit me like a wall. It was thick. Heavy, wrapping around my throat, it caused my stomach to twist. It almost drove me to my knees. The pounding of my heart flooded the space with the deafening, wild, erratic rhythm of grief and panic as I grunted out my pain.

The warmth of Gayle's blood clung to my hooves, a cruel reminder; the images of Gayle lying unresponsively on the pillow of green grass burned into my mind like branding fire. The twitch of Gayle's ears, the sound of her last word, run! The trauma didn't just leave a mark; it left a wound too deep to name.

The sound of another shot split the air like a thunderclap; the sound of rapid gunfire yanked Euley from the past, and terror consumed her soul. She turned not because she wanted to, but because she had to. A broken cry lodged in her throat as she fled, the ghost of Gayle's final breath. A terror so real lodged itself into her bones. From that moment on, every rustle in the trees, every snapped twig, became a whisper of death.

The hunter behind Euley was real; she had to flee from the physical threat. Each leap forward was an act of survival, but also of defiance. She was trying to outrun the belief that she was forever marked by pain, that her story would always be written by fear. Her trembling legs carried not just her body but the emotional weight of past losses, betrayals, and the invisible wounds left behind by trauma. This is why she ran, not just from the hunter, but from the memory of a friend she could not save.

The forest, alive with peril, became a mirror of her internal storm, thick, suffocating, and unpredictable. And yet, in this frantic flight, in every stride, there was the unspoken cry: Let me be free, not just from this chase, but from the captivity of everything I've endured.

CHAPTER THREE

The hunter methodically unloaded his gear; his mind rehearsing every step of his plan with calculated precision. His heart pounded with a primal rhythm, mirroring the adrenaline coursing through his veins. In his hands, the gun was more than a weapon; it was a bold declaration of intent, a symbol of his disregard for the rules meant to protect this sacred ground.

A defiant rule-breaker by nature, he was undeterred by the risks. His focus was singular and ruthless: to claim his target, no matter the cost or consequence. He personified the very thief Jesus warned of in John 10:10: "The thief comes only to steal and kill and destroy. . ." Every step he took echoed the darker side of that truth; the hunger for destruction, the craving to dominate and devour. His rifle was not merely a weapon of sport; it was the embodiment of a spirit that thrived on taking what was never his to claim.

Though the hunter thought himself master of the moment, what he could not see was that a greater Presence overshadowed the battlefield. The Shepherd of souls stood unseen, sovereign over both hunter and the hunted. His promises echoed louder than any rifle shot: life, not death; fullness, not fear.

His weapon of choice was a Savage Impulse Big Game Bolt-Action Rifle, loaded with two six-round magazines of .207 Winchester rounds; precision forged for lethal intent. This rifle had long been his trusted accomplice, a silent executioner that had delivered countless lives to the grave. At his side, rested his mistress of bloodshed: an old Desert Eagle blade, scarred from battle and heavy with history.

It was a grim keepsake from his final Army deployment, one

that ended not with honor, but with a dishonorable discharge for disorderly conduct. Together, these weapons told the story of a man who had long made peace with violence.

For this huntsman, the pursuit was never just about sustenance; it was the thrill of the kill that fueled him. He lived for the surge of adrenaline, the frantic cries of wounded prey, and the twisted satisfaction found in the spray of blood on forest leaves. Today's target was simple and deliberate: a deer. He had already envisioned the meal: tender venison steaks, roasted sweet corn, and buttered garlic potatoes; a feast fit for the centerpiece of his blood-stained gaming table.

Tomorrow night, the hunter would not dine alone. He had planned a gathering beneath the cold canopy of night, a silent communion of cunning and carnage. But these were no ordinary guests. They were not men, but beasts in form and nature: fox, sleek and sly with eyes like slivers of fire; wolf, loyal only to the scent of blood, his hunger never far from the surface; and coyote, the trickster, always circling, always watching, and laughing in the shadows before the strike.

They were his kind, predators not by necessity, but by design. Hunters of the weak, drawn together not by friendship, but by instinct, by the thrill of domination and the lust for control. There would be no ceremony, no warmth in their gathering, only meat, the taste of victory, and tales of the chase. And at the center of it all, the hunter would sit, relishing his role as provider. His pride fed not by the kill itself, but by the applause of those who lived to devour.

These were his friends with whom he had shared countless hours of poker, laughter, and drinks until dawn. Tonight, he would hunt for them. Tomorrow, they will feast. In his mind, he pictured the moment, bragging with smug satisfaction about how he had outwitted the park rangers once again. He licked his lips, savoring the thought of his own stealth and cunning, imagining himself not just as a hunter, but as a master craftsman of the kill. With a loud smack, he popped a fresh glob of tobacco into his mouth, already tasting the rich, roasted flavor of wild game, perfectly seasoned with Himalayan pink salt and cracked black pepper.

Turning away from his vehicle, which he had stashed deep within a low, hidden moth cave, its walls adorned with jagged stalagmites, dripping stalactites, and sheets of glistening flowstone, he moved with silent, predatory resolve. Every step was deliberate. Every breath focused. His pursuit had begun.

This calculating predator knew the rangers' patrol schedules down to the minute. He had spent weeks observing their routines, lurking in the shadows, patiently waiting for a breach in their defenses. Today, he had found it. It was Super Bowl Sunday, a national ritual where men, lost in drunken revelry, unleashed a year's worth of suppressed emotions under the guise of celebration.

And this devious hunter knew exactly what that kind of emotional chaos looked like. It was the one day of the year when even the most disciplined rangers let their guard down, distracted by team rivalries, trash talk, and bets that often escalated into shouting matches and scuffles. He counted on it. The frenzy of loyal fans, many of whom couldn't name more than three players on their chosen team, was his perfect cover.

The blaring music, slurred arguments, and bottomless drinks would create enough noise to drown out anything... even a gunshot. While they quarreled over touchdowns and penalties, he would strike with precision. The hunt was his game, and tonight, the field was wide open.

The Super Bowl Sunday spectacle provided the perfect camouflage for his meticulously planned hunt; this was his moment. Amid the chaos of celebration, no one would suspect a thing. The sharp crack of a rifle would blend effortlessly into the raucous chorus of slurred curses and triumphant cheers, masked by the blare of televisions and the clatter of beer bottles.

It was the perfect storm of distraction, giving him the cover he needed to strike, claim his prize, and disappear into the wilderness without a trace. A trivial game, insignificant compared to the value of a soul, served its purpose perfectly, a harmless distraction within the ranks that the hunter could exploit. He was that cunning predator. This was his plan, and the deer, whether she realized it or not, was just a pawn in his calculated scheme. She didn't stand a chance.

Several hundred yards away, a freshly painted red sign boldly declared "NO HUNTING ALLOWED." It's stark red and white lettering standing as a symbol of law and authority. But to the hunter, it was nothing more than a taunt, an empty threat flapping in the wind. His arrogance overshadowed any regard for rules or regulations. In his eyes, laws were made for the timid, for those too naive to grasp the raw, untamed truths of the world. He was a predator, unbound by boundaries, and no sign would dictate his will.

Just like the enemy of our souls that seeks to kill, steal, and destroy (John 10:10), a true predator doesn't follow rules; it dominates. And today, he would reign. His fingers twitched with anticipation. The familiar weight of his rifle was a cold comfort in his grip. His pulse quickened as he stepped into the clearing;

eyes narrowed, scanning the landscape for even the slightest motion.

Methodically, he strapped on his gear; each movement deliberate, practiced, almost ritualistic. The dull clink of metal buckles and the rasp of tightened straps broke the silence as he secured his pack. From the breast pocket of his green-and-brown camouflage overalls, he pulled out a small silver flask, worn smooth from years of use, and tucked it back in place; the gesture as natural to him as drawing breath.

A quick glance at his watch confirmed what he already knew: the timing was flawless. Every second mattered, and he prided himself on precision. His pulse quickened, not from fear, but from anticipation, as the moment he had rehearsed again and again finally arrived. Without a sound, he stepped forward, swallowed by the dense shadows of the woodland. The forest embraced him like an accomplice; its silence complicit in his mission. His boots pressed into the earth with careful precision; not a twig snapping, nor a leaf disturbed more than necessary. The scent of damp earth and moss filled his lungs, grounding him, sharpening his focus.

In his mind, there was only the hunt; no hesitation, no distraction, no second-guessing. His thoughts funneled into a singular, ruthless purpose: to claim his prize. The world around him seemed to fade until all that remained was the steady rhythm of his breath, the reassuring weight of his rifle, and the cold fire of intent burning behind his eyes.

Then, there she was. The doe. Young, unsuspecting, and utterly vulnerable. She stood just beyond the brush; a portrait of innocence painted against the wild. His muscles coiled, his breath slowed. He studied her every move, the subtle twitch of her ears, the delicate flare of her nostrils as she tested the wind.

He could almost taste her fear, thick in the air, sharp as iron, pulsing with the rhythm of her racing heart. It wasn't just imagined; it was real, tangible, vibrating through the silence like a drumbeat only he could hear. Each terrified breath, each frantic step called to him, matching the cadence of his own heartbeat until predator and prey seemed locked into one deadly rhythm.

She was close. Too close. The invisible tether between them grew tighter with every stride, drawing him nearer, pulling him into the inevitability of the strike. His pulse steadied as his mind sharpened, slipping into the cold focus he knew too well.

And in that moment, there was no hesitation, no mercy, only the ruthless precision of a killer who had practiced this dance too many times before. His hands, steady as stone. His eyes, unblinking. His body was coiled like a spring ready to release. He had ended lives before, and he would end another today. To him, it was no more than the execution of skill, deliberate, detached, and deadly.

He could almost feed on her fear, thick and metallic in the air, as if her terror itself was blood in his veins. She was close. Too close. And the nearness drove him mad with anticipation. His heartbeat slowed, but his hunger quickened, every nerve sharpened by obsession. His eyes narrowed, unblinking, fixed on the faintest trace of her movement. His grip on the rifle was tender, almost reverent, as though it were an extension of his own will, his own dark craving made flesh and steel.

A shiver of ecstasy ran down his spine at the thought of her collapse, the spray of life against the grass, the silence that always followed. He lived for that silence, the holy hush after the kill. It was not food he sought, not sustenance. It was dominion. It was a conquest. It was power.

And now, with every step, he moved not like a man, but like something more primal, more sinister. A creature enthralled by the kill, enslaved to its rush. In his mind, he had already claimed her. The forest was merely the stage and he, the executioner.

CHAPTER FOUR

Unaware of the danger creeping ever closer, Euley lingered in the quiet beauty of the glade; her slender neck bent low as she nibbled at a cluster of ripe raspberries. Their sweetness burst against her tongue, filling her with a sense of simple joy. The sunlight poured gently through the canopy, scattering golden flecks across her back like a blessing, while the hum of summer wrapped the forest in a lullaby of warmth.

For a lingering moment, the world felt safe, whole, as though the pain of her past had been swallowed up by this sanctuary of berries and birdsong. Her ears twitched lazily at the buzz of a dragonfly; her tail flicked in rhythm with the whisper of the breeze. She was content. She was free. But then, something shifted. Subtle, almost imperceptible. The kind of disturbance that prickled at the edges of instinct.

A whisper in the wind that did not belong. The raspberries lost their sweetness on her tongue as unease began to seep in. The stillness of the forest grew too heavy, too complete, like a blanket pressed too tightly against the skin.

Her ears flicked again, sharper this time. Her muscles tensed. Somewhere, just beyond sight, the balance had tilted. The air carried not just the fragrance of summer, but a warning.

Instinct kicked in. She froze mid-step, her ears twitching, her head lifted high as her amber eyes scanned the treelined area. The forest, once serene, now felt unsettled. And then, without warning, the unexpected happened.

The first shot shattered the silence, ripping through the forest with a thunderous crack that echoed like a warning bell across the trees. Birds scattered in panicked flurries, their wings thrashing against the sky. The ground itself seemed to tremble beneath the violence of the sound.

But she didn't fall.

Euley stood where she was, frozen, yet unbroken. Her legs locked. Her body taut with instinct. Every muscle quivering in the aftershock, but she remained upright. She didn't buckle. She didn't collapse. Not as he had expected. Her chest heaved, nostrils flared, eyes wide and luminous, reflecting both terror and defiance. She looked almost statuesque, an image of fragile beauty framed against the chaos of the moment, yet held by some unseen force that refused to let her topple. It was as if the very words of the prophet were echoing through the forest: "No weapon formed against you shall prosper" (Isaiah 54:17).

The hunter's jaw clenched. Confusion surged through him, mingled with anger, a hot ember in his gut. He had been so sure, so precise. His bullet should have claimed her. But there she stood, untouched, unyielding. Doubt crept into his mind, replacing the triumph he had already begun to taste.

In that breathless span of time, the balance of the hunt shifted. It was no longer just about the kill. Something greater had stepped into the space between predator and prey, and the forest itself seemed to recognize it.

A sudden shift in the air jolted the fawn's instincts; she sensed it. She was being hunted. Her body went rigid, every muscle tightening as a surge of fear coursed through her. Her mind screamed, "Run! Danger!" but her legs betrayed her, frozen in place. The serenity of the moment had been violently shattered by the unmistakable crack of gunfire, a sound she had heard before and never forgotten.

Paralyzed between instinct and terror, she stood trembling, caught in the cruel grip of fear and trauma. The memory crashed into her like a storm, and though the years had passed, the pain had never left. It lived beneath the surface, waiting to emerge, just like now. Silently wordlessly, Psalm 34:4 welled up from the depth of her soul, "I sought the Lord, and he answered me; he delivered me from all my fears."

As if nature itself had orchestrated the moment, the urgent bleats and distressed grunts of nearby fawns sliced through the fog of Euley's mind. Their cries, sharp and desperate, jolted her back to the present, just in time. Another round of whistling gunfire ripped through the air, bullets tearing past her in rapid succession.

The sharp, staccato cracks of the rifle sent shockwaves through her; each shot intensifying the trauma reverberating in her soul. It wasn't just noise; it was a trigger, reopening wounds she thought had scarred over. The forest around her blurred as survival instinct surged forward, crashing over the weight of memory. She had to move. Now.

With every ounce of will, Euley fought to command her trembling legs to respond. The memory of Gayle's dried blood, once soaked into the earth and now etched forever in Euley's soul, pulsed beneath her hooves like a silent scream. Grief warped into panic as the horrifying truth settled in, the hunter wasn't just near, he was coming for her. He wouldn't stop. He was determined to end her life just as he had likely stolen countless others.

Then, BANG, another single, deafening shot exploded through the silence, and something inside her broke free. Her legs unrooted from the ground with a force she didn't know she possessed. Her mind roared with urgency, "Run! And with that, she flew through brush, through pain, through memory, fighting for life Gayle never had the chance to keep.

The violent crack of the rifle detonated in the air, unleashing a tidal wave of panic that surged through Euley's body. Her heart thundered with such force that it felt as if it might explode from her chest. The sound wasn't just noise; it was war. It shattered her breath, tightened her chest, and sent her mind spiraling into a storm of fear.

Instinct ignited like fire. With the grace of a gymnast and the desperation of the hunted, she pivoted sharply and launched into a full sprint across the open field. But this wasn't a mere flight; it was survival. Every muscle burned, every breath rasped like fire in her lungs, but she didn't stop. She couldn't. She was no longer just a deer fleeing a predator; she was a soul running from the weight of memory, from terror, from death itself.

The bullets missed, but barely. Too close for comfort, and far too close for pride. Adrenaline surged hot in the hunter's veins, quickly overtaken by a rising tide of rage. How dare she escape me? His jaw clenched, teeth grinding with frustration as his grip tightened around the weapon.

This was no longer just a hunt. It had become personal.

She was no longer just a deer; she was defiance incarnate, a moving target that challenged his skill, his dominance, his ego. She had become a living riddle, and he was obsessed with the answer. This chase was never just about the meat, but it had evolved into an even more delectable conquest. And he wouldn't stop until she fell.

Her only objective was FREEDOM. LIFE. Euley wanted to

live. Every fiber of her being screamed for survival. She refused to die, not like Gayle, not today. But the hunter was fast, relentless, and cruelly skilled. No matter how desperately she weaved and darted through the trees, she couldn't shake him.

Gunfire rang out behind her, bullets slicing through the air; each one a near miss. Then, a single shot, a gleaming silver slug, fired at deadly close range, aimed with chilling precision at her heart. It should have ended her. But by a miracle, it missed. By a breath, by a hair, it slammed into a nearby tree with a violent thud.

The impact sent a shock wave through her. Her heart seized in terror, her legs faltered, and a piercing pressure surged through her ears, threatening to pull her under. For a split second, she stumbled on the verge of collapse.

The closeness of death ignited her will. Drawing from a place deeper than instinct, deeper than fear, Euley forced her body forward, her soul roaring louder than the chase behind her. She would not be taken. Not now. Not ever.

He pursued her with the relentless focus of a trained predator; each stride sharp and calculated, his body moving with the efficiency of an elite CrossFit warrior. The gap between them narrowed with every heartbeat. And yet, something was off.

Shifting his rifle, once a trusted extension of his control, only deepened his frustration. It no longer felt like an advantage; it felt like a burden. The doe, Euley, was proving far more cunning than he anticipated. She weaved through the trees with instinctual brilliance, turning the forest into a maze that mocked his precision.

Each missed shot clawed at his pride. This wasn't how it was supposed to go. He knew this game. He had dominated it for years. He understood its rhythms, its rules. But she was just a wild, untamed animal. She wasn't supposed to outsmart him. And yet, she did, but he was convinced that she couldn't keep it up forever. Sooner or later, she'd falter. And when she did, he would be there, ready to end the chase.

The chase reached a fever pitch as another long-range bullet cut through the air, silent, swift, and deadly. It missed her by inches, but the rush of wind against her flank caused the short hair on her hide to bristle in alarm. Terror surged, but so did memory.

In a split second, Euley remembered a hidden shelter, nestled near the berry patch, a sacred hollow carved into the earth like a secret sanctuary. It was no ordinary place. It had been heaved out by the hands of God Himself, the Creator, Elohim, a shelter where fear had no voice. With renewed hope, she shifted direction, her hooves pounding the ground with urgency.

In her moment of fear and desperation, Psalm 91:1–2 "He who dwells in the secret place of the Most High shall abide under the shadow of the Almighty. I will say of the Lord, 'He is my refuge and my fortress; My God, in Him I will trust.", becomes a manifestation of God's promise to protect and cover those who trust in Him.

Behind her, the hunter adjusted his strategy. Strapping his rifle bag securely over both shoulders, he lifted his knees and broke into a full sprint, calling on every ounce of strength and agility. His breath was sharp, labored. He pushed harder.

But the forest, once neutral, seemed to rise against him.

Vines snagged at his boots, thorns clawed his arms, and the

underbrush swallowed his path. Every step became a struggle. His rifle, once a symbol of control and power, now dragged him on like dead weight. The deeper he pursued, the more the woods resisted, as if creation itself was conspiring to protect the fawn from the hunter.

Nature knows and honors its creator, responding to protect what belongs to Him. Job 12:7-10 "But ask the animals, and they will teach you, or the birds in the sky, and they will tell you; or speak to the earth, and it will teach you, or let the fish in the sea inform you. Which of all these does not know that the hand of the Lord has done this? In His hand is the life of every creature and the breath of all mankind." The forest became a divine instrument, defending the innocent and frustrating the plans of destruction.

The hunter muttered a string of curses under his breath, his voice low and venomous; each word bitten off like it could somehow cut through his frustration. Sweat ran down his temples, stinging his eyes, as the weight of his lightweight, custom-made gear clung to him like an anchor. It was designed to make him faster, sharper, untouchable, a predator among predators. But now, the straps dug into his shoulders, the rifle dragged against his back, and every step felt like he was trudging through quicksand. The very gear meant to give him the edge was betraying him, mocking him with every labored breath.

And yet, there she was. Through the blur of sweat and shadow, he caught sight of her, a fragile silhouette framed by the tangle of vines and dappled light. His pulse quickened, pupils narrowing as his sights locked on her. To him, she wasn't just a creature anymore. She was a prize. Dinner. Victory. His redemption from failure.

She stood only a heartbeat away, close enough for him to taste the triumph on his tongue, close enough that he imagined the weight of her body dropping against the earth. The hunger in his gut twisted into obsession, his mind already feasting on the kill even before the trigger was pulled. Every nerve screamed with anticipation. He adjusted his grip, steadying his aim. This would be it. The moment of conquest.

CHAPTER FIVE

Euley stood trapped, her slender foot ensnared in a cruel tangle of love vines that coiled like serpents around her ankle. Each frantic tug only made the snare constrict tighter; the green tendrils digging into her hide with merciless strength. Panic surged through her body like fire racing through dry grass, every nerve sparking with terror.

Her prized right ankle, the very limb that had carried her through ten miles of flight, now throbbed under the pressure, threatening to snap with every desperate jerk. She thrashed, her chest heaving, nostrils flaring, but the vines only bit deeper, twisting as if the forest itself conspired to hold her fast. Her heart pounded violently, echoing in her ears like a war drum. The air around her seemed to grow heavier, suffocating, as the reality settled in, she was caught. Helpless. Exposed. A living target waiting for the hunter's silver bullet.

Terror stole her breath, but it was more than fear of death that gripped her. Memories of Gayle's blood pooling into the earth came rushing back; each image stabbing her heart with grief. She could already see her friend's lifeless body in her mind's eye, and now she braced herself to become the next to fall. The forest that once offered berries and refuge now felt like a cage, its shadows closing in. Every muscle screamed for freedom, but the vines mocked her struggle. She was no longer running. She was waiting for the hunter, for the shot, for the end.

Memories of Gayle's death crashed over me with violent clarity, as if time itself had torn open. I saw her again, motionless and breathless. Her fragile body crumpled at my hooves; her once-bright eyes staring into nothing, wide and empty. The sight burned into my soul like fire on dry wood.

Her blood... oh, her blood. It soaked into the soft earth like a sacred offering, a dark crimson stream flowing between my hooves, carrying away the life we had shared only moments before. Its scent was iron and sorrowful, unforgettable, indelible, rising in the air like a ghost I could never outrun.

I stood frozen. Every muscle in my body locked tight, gripped by invisible chains of terror. My breath caught in my throat, shallow, ragged; my chest heaving against a rising tide of anguish and despair. My mind screamed at me to run, but my legs refused, weighed down by grief and fear. In that moment, time did not move. It was just me, the blood, and the silence of death echoing in my soul.

I could feel the bullet before it ever came, the phantom pain of what I believed would surely be my end. My heart pounded like a war drum inside my ribs; each beat screaming that this was it. This was how it ended. The fear was suffocating, the trauma unrelenting. I braced myself, waiting for the sharp eruption of pain, the final silence that would swallow me whole. And yet, even there, even then, I remembered... "The Lord is close to the brokenhearted and saves those who are crushed in spirit." (Psalm 34:18)

The air pressed heavily in my lungs, suffocating me. Fear coiled tightly around my throat like a serpent, stealing every breath, choking out reason. My body trembled, bracing for the eruption of pain, the tearing of flesh, the silence that would swallow me whole. The trauma of Gayle's death flashed like lightning before my eyes, her lifeless form a cruel reminder of what was coming for me. My spirit quaked, my hope wavered, and despair crept into the cracks of my soul.

And yet, even there, even then, a rising reiteration above the storm of panic, quiet but unshakable: "The Lord is close to the brokenhearted and saves those who are crushed in spirit." (Psalm 34:18). The words came like a balm, a whisper of truth in the chaos. Tears burned in my eyes, but with them came something unexpected, a flicker of hope. If the Lord was near to the brokenhearted, then He was near to me now, here in this moment of terror. If He saves the crushed in spirit, then maybe, just maybe, this wasn't the end after all.

In the tension between death's shadow and divine promise, I trembled, but I did not collapse. Somewhere deep within, where reason and strength had long since fled, a still small voice spoke louder than the terror. "When you pass through the waters, I will be with you; and through the rivers, they shall not overflow you. When you walk through the fire, you shall not be burned." (Isaiah 43:2) The words rose up like a shield around me. I was not alone. I had never been. My tears became prayers. My breath, though unsteady, became praise. I wasn't just standing in the shadow of death, I was standing in the presence of the Deliverer. And I knew that what was meant to destroy me, would not have the final say.

CHAPTER SIX

The forest held its breath. Shadows stretched long across the ground as the last rays of sun slipped through the canopy, casting slivers of gold and green over the tangled undergrowth. Somewhere, a brook murmured softly, its sound swallowed by an ominous quiet. Every rustle of leaves, every whisper of wind felt weighted, as though the woods themselves sensed what was about to unfold. Danger prowled just beyond the edge of sight, unseen, but undeniable, pressing in like a storm about to break.

The sound of footsteps closed in, heavy, sure, relentless. Each thud against the earth reverberated through the trees like a drumbeat of doom. The hunter moved with calculated precision, aligning his body behind a curtain of brush. His eyes narrowed, glinting with cold satisfaction as he spotted his target. His breath slowed, each inhale deliberate, trained to remain undisturbed even in the thrill of the kill.

Time seemed to stretch as he lifted the rifle, the metal cool and familiar in his hands. Every muscle in his body stilled; every nerve attuned to that singular moment. He found her. There she was, vulnerable, unaware, trembling from exhaustion.

The barrel of the rifle locked onto her fragile form, steady and unflinching. Cold steel against warm flesh, death aimed straight at life. There was no warning, no pause for hesitation, no shred of mercy lingering in the hunter's heart.

His breath slowed, practiced, controlled; each inhale and exhale honed by countless hunts before. The world narrowed to a single point: her. Everything else blurred, the whisper of the leaves, the hum of the brook, even the pounding of his own blood in his ears. All that remained was the target.

His finger curled around the trigger with chilling familiarity, the ease of one who had done this a hundred times, a thousand. The motion was almost tender, reverent even, as though pulling the trigger was not an act of violence but of ecclesiastical ritual. For him, this was worship, the offering of power, the thrill of dominion.

And then, he fired.

The explosion tore through the silence, a thunderclap that split the air in two. The recoil jolted his shoulder; the echo ricocheted through the forest, scattering birds into frantic flight. The bullet screamed through the air, slicing time itself, a silver streak carrying the weight of death in its path.

For Euley, the world slowed.

The merciless echo thundered through the trees, scattering the stillness into chaos. She could almost feel it coming, the phantom burn across her chest, the finality chasing her in that instant. Fear and faith collided inside her soul. The violence tore through the moment, leaving the air congealed with smoke and consequences.

Time slowed to a sluggish crawl with each heartbeat stretching into eternity. The bullet roared through the air, invisible yet undeniable, closing the gap between predator and prey. But even before the echo of the gunfire had finished tearing through the forest, something stirred in the hunter's chest. It wasn't the predicted triumph. It wasn't the relied upon satisfaction. It was a deep unease that slithered beneath his ribs; a tremor of something he could not name. His breath hitched, his certainty faltered. Because what he saw next… was not what he expected.

The smoke still curled from the barrel of his rifle, but the scene before him refused to align with his intent. Euley did not collapse into the earth. She did not crumble as prey before the predator. Instead, she stood, trembling yet unbroken, her wide eyes glistening with something stronger than fear. Her body was framed in a shaft of golden light that pierced through the canopy, casting her not as a victim, but as something almost untouchable, sacred.

The forest itself seemed to rise in her defense. The wind hushed, the leaves whispered, and the brook's song deepened, as though heaven and earth had bent low to shield her. The hunter's pulse quickened, not with the thrill of conquest, but with dread. He felt it now, he perceived it: he was no longer in control. The power in that place belonged to another.

In the same instant, Euley threw her head back, her eyes wide with terror and desperation. From the depths of her chest rose a raw, aching cry, a sound born from growing, surging, soaring faith. It tore through the forest like a sacred plea, a final, desperate call to the One who had formed her, the only One who could rescue her from the shadow of death.

It was not a cry the human ear could interpret, but heaven understood. Creation stood still, as if pausing to witness her prayers. "Then they cried to the Lord in their trouble, and He saved them from their distress. He sent out His word and healed them; He rescued them from the grave." (Psalm 107:19–20) In that moment, her voice met mercy, and mercy answered.

Euley's cry erupted through the woodland like a primal wail that echoed with such force, it felt as if the very trees shuddered. The sound boomeranged through the air, loud as a bullhorn, cutting through chaos like a blade. The power of her cry startled the hunter; his gun slipped from the sling, clattering awkwardly against his side.

Everything fell still.

CHAPTER SEVEN

The forest no longer felt ordinary; it pulsed with an invisible weight, a presence palpable enough to sense. The hunter stepped forward, unaware that he was crossing from the realm of the natural world into something wholly other. The shadows deepened, the air pressed heavy against his chest, and the atmosphere shifted as if unseen eyes were watching, waiting. Every instinct in his body screamed that this was no longer just a hunt; it was an encounter. Something sacred, something terrifying, had awakened in the woods.

A strange, sharp scent of cedar suddenly filled the space; so strong, it made him choke on his chewing tobacco. His body tensed, the hair on his arms standing upright as a chill crawled down his spine. The moment felt suspended, unreal, and almost cinematic, as if he had stepped into something far beyond his human comprehension. His hand trembled as he fumbled for the canister at his side, desperation drying out his throat. He took a long, greedy gulp, the water sliding down like gravel against his parched nerves. Sweat clung to his brow, his heart thundering in his chest as he tried to outpace the chaos rising in his mind.

And then he blinked, hard. He couldn't believe what his eyes were telling him. Just two feet ahead, the deer hadn't fallen at all. Instead, she twisted and bucked wildly, confusion etched in every frantic movement. Her hooves struck the ground with desperate force, scattering leaves and dirt into the air. She should have been down, finished. But she wasn't. She was alive, resisting, fighting against the death he thought he had sealed.

She should have been dead. The boom of the rifle still echoed in her ears, the smell of gunpowder clinging to the air like a curse. Yet she stood, shaking, trembling, but alive. Confusion surged through her veins like ice and fire, her heart pounding so violently it felt as if it would tear free. Her legs quivered beneath her, bracing for a collapse that never came.

Her eyes locked onto the hunter, wide, glassy, glistening with terror yet shimmering with something ancient, something unbroken: pain, defiance, survival. She didn't understand why she was still breathing, why she still felt the earth beneath her hooves.

Like a seasoned warrior, forged by countless hunts, the hunter moved with a chilling calm. His steps were silent, calculated, as if the earth itself feared to betray his presence. His eyes, sharp and cold, swept the terrain with a predator's focus; each movement a rehearsed reprisal of violence. Every breath he took was measured; every heartbeat synchronized with the rhythm of the chase. There was no hesitation in his hands, only a lethal certainty born from years of mastering the art of pursuit.

He had fired his last shot, not just of the day, but of his pride, his control, his sense of dominion over the wild. And for a fleeting moment, time fractured, suspended in the split-second between intent and impact, where fate held its breath and destiny prepared to turn.

Her eyes, wide, wild, and glistening, mirrored both terror and innocence, two pools of light that pierced straight through him, stripping him of his confidence. They were not just eyes; they were weapons of truth, reflecting every shadow of fear and every fragile thread of hope all at once.

The air between them seemed to crackle, charged with an unseen electricity. Time slowed. Even the forest fell silent, as though creation itself held its breath. It was then the words rose in her spirit like a lifeline: "I shall not die, but live, and declare the works of the Lord." (Psalm 118:17). The verse echoed inside her like thunder, drowning out the echo of the shot, reminding her that this moment was not her end, but the beginning of her testimony.

And then she moved, sudden, fluid, desperate, her body twisting away from the line of fire with the grace of a ballerina mid-turn. Her hooves carved the earth as if it were a stage. Each motion born not of art, but of survival; a dance choreographed by instinct and terror. She spun, trembling yet elegant, a fragile figure whirling in defiance of death itself. The vines that held her ankles earlier had loosened their grip. The hunter's breath caught. For a split second, it was no longer predator against prey, but man staring into the raw, unbroken spirit of creation itself.

The forest answered with silence, not the peaceful kind, but the kind that rings in ears and presses against chests. No birds called. No branches creaked. Even the winds refused to whistle. Throwing his gun to the ground, yanking his blade from the sheath, he postured his body to run towards his prey; then, the resistance began. Vines slithered like perceptively active things across his boots, catching and tightening with each step. Brambles reached out like claws, tearing at his sleeves and dragging against his skin. Every step forward felt like a trespass, as if nature were concertedly fighting against him.

His breath grew ragged. More sweat trickled down his temple, now mingling with the sting of small cuts. The ground beneath his feet felt unsteady, alive, and unwilling to let him pass.

It was no longer a pursuit. It was a warning. The woods weren't just sheltering the prey. They were protecting her.

Still, adrenaline drowned out doubt. Driven by the intoxication of conquest, he hurriedly adjusted his weapon in his left hand while licking his lips with anticipation. With heart pounding and footsteps heavy, he charged full speed toward the animal, ready to conquer, but starkly unaware that he was racing toward a moment far greater than the kill.

As she pivoted in midair, Euley caught the hunter in her peripheral vision, his figure looming like a shadow carved from death itself. The sight sent a jolt of terror racing down her spine, her heart hammering so hard it rattled her chest. The shock of the moment was unbearable, her world narrowing to the glint of steel and the steady aim of destruction.

Her traumatized body betrayed her, muscles seizing, hooves stumbling as if the weight of every memory dragged her down. Her soul was caught, snared in the grip of fear so suffocating it seemed to strangle the very breath from her lungs. For one suspended heartbeat, she hung between flight and collapse, strength and surrender. Her spirit cried out for freedom, but terror and trauma chained her limbs. She was prey, trembling at the edge of destiny.

Time felt frozen, wavering between life and death. But what she didn't know was that the tides had quickly turned. An unseen force had stepped onto the battlefield, a divine presence, moved between her and the threat, subtly tipping the scales in her favor.

In the blink of an eye, everything shifted.

"When the enemy comes in like a flood, the Spirit of the Lord will lift up a standard against him." (Isaiah 59:19). In that sacred instant, what looked like the end became the turning point. And in that sacred instant, what seemed like the end became a powerful, new beginning. What the enemy meant for destruction, God intercepted with deliverance.

She wasn't alone. Heaven had heard her cry and help had come. A surge of supernatural strength coursed through her, not from within, but from above. It wrapped around her like a mantle, igniting her weary limbs with power not her own.

Instinctively, Euley leapt forward with the grace and strength of a regal gymnast, bold, fearless, and free. No longer restrained, she darted through the dense forest, her hooves skimming the earth as if she were flying, not fleeing. Her mind raced in tandem with her body, thoughts pounding to the same furious rhythm as her heart, a relentless drumbeat of survival. "Keep going," she urged herself, breath ragged, panic rising. "Don't stop. Not now. He's close… too close."

The hunter's presence loomed behind her, a heavy, suffocating shadow that threatened to devour her with every step. "Why won't he stop?" she cried inwardly, despair pressing hard against her chest. "What have I done to deserve this?"

The question burned through her as fiercely as the ache in her legs. But there was no time for answers. Only the will to survive. Her legs burned with exhaustion, each stride slower than the last as the relentless chase drained her strength. Her body screamed for rest, but there was no time, only the echo of danger behind her. Tears welled, but she pushed them down. "Survive now," she whispered to herself, clenching her jaw. "You can mourn later."

But the sorrow clung to her like a shadow, an unseen chain tugging at her spirit, threatening to pull her under even as she fought to run free. The weight of mourning was heavy, but her will to live was heavier.

The predator had lost control of the game. With the wind pressing on her back like a whisper of encouragement, Euley surged forward, unknowingly guiding the hunter into unfamiliar ground. The chase veered into a dense, untamed stretch of forest, an ancient place thick with secrets.

Low-lying shrubs clawed at her legs, while tangled vines wove a treacherous web across the forest floor. Towering trees with wide, shadow-casting leaves loomed above, forming a canopy so dense that sunlight barely touched the earth. Every step pulled them both deeper into the unknown, where even the hunter's confidence began to waver.

The thought gnawed at him, biting into his pride like a festering wound. He could still hear her, hooves tapping lightly in the distance, quick and rhythmic, as if she were no longer of this world but gliding into some unseen realm.

The forest, once his domain, now roared with unfamiliar sounds, leaves rustling like whispers, branches creaking like warnings. His heart pounded violently against his ribs, and the sweat slicking his brow was no longer just from the chase. It was something deeper. Unsettling. Spiritual.

CHAPTER EIGHT

A shift had occurred. He could feel it. The rules had changed. And in that moment, with breath shallow and pulse erratic, he realized the truth: he was no longer the hunter. He was being pursued by something far greater than himself.

For the first time in years, doubt gripped him. Was he ever truly in control? The question echoed in his mind like a warning bell. He looked around, disoriented, as the fawn vanished beyond his reach, slipping through his fingers like smoke. The very landscape that once fueled his dominance, now felt foreign, unfamiliar, almost hostile. The forest no longer welcomed him; it watched him.

Something had shifted.

The thrill that once surged through him had dissolved, replaced by a cold, creeping unease that settled in his bones. The hunt was no longer a game. It was a reckoning.

When he finally came to a halt, lungs burning and chest heaving, the forest had fallen into an eerie stillness. The thrill that once surged through his veins had vanished, leaving behind only the echo of fading footsteps and the hollow thump of his slowing heartbeat. The deer, his prize, was gone, swallowed by the shadows of the trees.

He stood there, alone. The anger that once drove him now unraveling into a quiet, gnawing frustration. But this felt like more than a missed shot. It was a rupture, an unraveling of something deeper. This wasn't just the loss of a kill. It was the loss of control.

A poignant realization crept in that the hunter had become

the hunted. Not in the way he understood with guns and prey, but in spirit, the power had shifted. And somewhere, deep in his gut, he wondered if the chase had ever truly been about the kill at all. Maybe it was about revealing what hunted him, his own hunger for domination, and his misplaced power; deep in his gut, he felt it: conviction. A silent whisper that perhaps it was time for him to change his focus.

With his bullets spent and his target vanished, the hunter's meticulously crafted vision unraveled before him. What had once felt like a calculated pursuit now devolved into chaos, like a competition whose rules had shifted in the final round. His confidence, once unshakable, gave way to frustration, rising hot and bitter in his dark, predatory soul.

He stood there, gripping his empty weapon, surrounded by the silence of a forest that no longer answered him. The terrain he once commanded now felt unyielding, almost sacred, as if something greater had intervened. Something unseen. Something ancient. A force beyond the laws he knew, beyond the world he thought he could conquer. And for the first time, he wondered if he had been trespassing not just on protected land, but on holy ground.

Euley's breath came in short, ragged gasps, her chest heaving with exhaustion. Her throat burned, dry and raw, as if scorched by the fear she carried. The thought of water shimmered in her mind, a memory more than a promise.

The stream. If she could just reach the stream. "I need it... I must get there," she pleaded inwardly, pushing her aching body forward. But doubt slithered through her thoughts, cold and relentless. "What if you don't make it? What if you're too late?" These questions echoed like a shadow behind her resolve, yet still, she pressed on, chasing hope, one desperate stride at

Euley's focus shifted inward. Her breath was ragged, her muscles screaming, but a deeper ache began to surface, one not born of exhaustion, but of weariness in spirit. "Why do I keep running?" she wondered. "What is the purpose of this struggle? Am I fighting for life… or simply delaying the inevitable?" In that shadowed moment, when fear threatened to swallow her whole, a gentle echo rose from the depths of her soul, a whisper of something sacred, long buried, but never forgotten:

"As the deer pants for streams of water, so my soul pants for You, my God." (Psalm 42:1)

The words wrapped around her like a warm cloak in the cold. They weren't just scripture; they were memory, melody, and meaning. The darkness didn't disappear, but it lost its grip. With each stride, the sacred lullaby continued, weaving through the wind: "He who dwells in the secret place of the Most High shall abide under the shadow of the Almighty."(Psalms 91:1)

And as her hooves beat the earth, Euley wasn't just running from death; she was running toward refuge. Toward promise. Toward the One who had never left her side.

Compelled by a singular, aching need to plunge into cool water and quench the fire in her throat, Euley pushed deeper into the heart of the forest. It had been hours since her last drink, and the thirst now clawed at her insides with relentless urgency. Each step felt heavier, her body weary, but her spirit refused to surrender.

The raw heat of trauma still burned in her chest, a silent rage smoldering beneath the surface. Yet, even as pain gnawed at her resolve, she pressed on, fueled not only by survival but by sheer, unyielding will. In the face of death, she chose to keep moving. Not because it was easy, but because she had to. Because something within her still believed the water was near… and with it, the hope of life.

CHAPTER NINE

With her nose tilted northward, Euley galloped toward the sacred place, the sweet, earthy scent of water riding the thick, humid air. Each breath drew her closer to what her soul craved: refreshment, safety and the presence of peace. She could feel it and she knew she was near. But her strength was waning and her spirit teetered on the edge of collapse.

Still, she pressed on.

Veering off the familiar path, Euley navigated the forest with instinct sharpened by desperation. Her hooves barely touched the ground as she moved, the trees around her blurring into streaks of green and gold. The urgency of survival fueled her, driving her beyond exhaustion.

And then, there it was.

The stream shimmered under the midday light, bordered by broad-leaf foliage that arched overhead, forming a sanctuary of shadow and stillness.

Without hesitation, she plunged headfirst into the water, the cool embrace washing over her like a baptism. Her legs buckled beneath her, surrendering at last to exhaustion. Hidden beneath the veil of overhanging shrubs, she collapsed into the stream, heart pounding with relief. Safe, at least for now. Grateful for the cover, she lay still, cloaked in the forest's grace, her predator left searching in vain.

Euley collapsed, trembling from sheer exhaustion. Her limbs quaked beneath her, every muscle aching, with trembling lips, she drank deeply. The cool water flowing over her tongue like a healing balm, seeping into the cracks of her parched soul. Each swallow pulled the rich silt and minerals from the stream, earth's quiet offering to the broken and weary.

The water satisfied more than just her thirst; it washed over the fear, the trauma, the weight of the chase, and the lingering sorrow of Gayle's death. It rinsed away the invisible stains that clung to her like a second skin, until all that remained was surrender.

Immersed in the stream's gentle current, Euley let go. She released the terror, the struggle and her pain to her Creator, the One who had seen her, shielded her and sustained her. With a heart full of gratitude, she offered a silent thanks for the life she still held… for the value He had placed on her existence.

In that precious moment, the forest seemed to fall still, as if all of creation paused to witness the offering. And Euley felt it, not the presence of her pursuer, but something far greater. Divine. Holy. El Shaddai.

The sun broke through the canopy above, casting golden rays that shimmered on the surface of the water. The leaves rustled in harmony, their honeysuckle-sweet song a quiet serenade, announcing that God was nearby. Her heart calmed, her breath deepened, and for the first time in what felt like forever, Euley felt safe. Seen. Held.

A tremble of relief rippled down her spine as Euley bowed her head once more, overcome with gratitude. Her heart swelled with awe, tears brimming in her eyes, not of sorrow, but of sincere recognition. "You are here," she breathed inwardly, the words resting softly in her spirit. "You have not forgotten me."

The water that touched her lips was more than refreshing; it was holy. A baptism. A sacred washing away of the terror, grief and sorrow that had wrapped themselves around her like chains. In its cool embrace, fear loosened its grip and pain began to dissolve into something unexplainable, peace.

The heaviness lifted.

The silence around her became a sanctuary and her soul, once rattled by panic, now stood still in the presence of the Divine. "You are my shield," she whispered, her voice no louder than the breeze. "My Savior… and my God."

In the sacred stillness, a gentle voice stirred within Euley's spirit, a whisper, not of fear, but of reassurance: "Why, my soul, are you downcast? Why so disturbed within me? Put your hope in God, for I will yet praise Him, my Savior and my God." The ancient words of Psalm 42 echoed through her, like a melody being carried on the wind, soft, but powerful.

In that moment, something shifted.

Fear gave way to faith. The trembling in her limbs stilled. The storm inside her heart calmed. She understood, deeply, unshakably, that though the hunter had pursued her flesh, he could never possess her soul. It belonged to the One who had formed her, breathed life into her and watched over her even in the darkest hour. Her spirit was not prey; it was a promise. And it was eternally His.

Rising from the stream, Euley felt strength surge through her, not just in body, but in spirit. She was no longer merely a victim of the hunt; she was a survivor, a living testament to the mercy and might of her Creator. Each droplet of water that clung to her fur shimmered like a seal of divine protection, a reminder that she had been spared.

As she stepped toward the coppice, her stride held a new purpose. Gratitude flowed through her like a quiet river, steady and sure. No longer was she running from fear; she was moving forward with hope. The hunter's shadow still lingered at the edges of the forest, however, he no longer claim her thoughts or peace.

Euley's heart swelled with profound gratitude for the gift of a second chance. The water had done more than quench her thirst; it had cleansed her of fear, lifting the weight of trauma from her body, mind and soul. She stood renewed, in that golden stillness, she felt it, an unseen presence gently guiding her, not with force, but with love. It led her toward repentance, not in shame, but in grace. Toward healing, not in silence, but in the sacred hush of peace. Tranquility seeped into the deepest parts of her being, whispering a quiet strength that steadied her steps.

CHAPTER TEN

Guided by a divine Spirit, Euley quieted herself, sinking deeper into the shelter of the dense green foliage where sunlight barely pierced the canopy. Hidden, breath held, and body still, she watched in silence as the hunter, defeated and weary, lowered his head, shifting his weapons and pounding his chest as he walked away. There was no victory in his stride, only defeat.

In that majestic hush, a familiar phrase drifted across her mind like a gentle breeze: *"Be still and know that I am God."*

Peace washed over her like a quiet tide, and without speaking, Euley lifted her eyes toward the heavens. *"Thank You, Master,"* her soul whispered. No words were needed. She was safe and held in the hands of the One who never failed. As Euley bowed her head in silent reverence, her chest rose and pulsed something greater: Awe, Deliverance, Grace. Lifting her weary eyes to the heavens again, her lips parted and from the depths of her soul, a song of gratitude arose, authentic, unfiltered, and achingly beautiful.

Her voice trembled at first, fragile as a reed in the wind. But with each note, strength returned, and her melody grew bolder, a song of thanksgiving to the Lord of her salvation. It wasn't rehearsed or polished, but it was pure. Holy.

The forest fall still in hallowed attention. The wind carried her song like a blessed offering, rustling the leaves in gentle agreement. The brook, once a soft murmur, now bubbled with a peaceful rhythm, as if echoing her praise. High above, birds joined in, their chirps and calls weaving through the trees like nature's own hallelujah and amen.

And as the golden sun dipped low, spilling warm light across the woodland floor, the entire forest exhaled. Wrapped in its glow, Euley stood surrounded by peace, by presence and by the quiet joy of knowing she had been spared. Heaven and earth had heard her song. And they rejoiced with her.

Gathering herself, Euley drew in a long, steady breath, letting it anchor her as the tension slowly melted from her limbs. Peace settled where panic had once reigned. Lifting her head, she opened her eyes to the fading light, casting a warm glow across her face. The fear and exhaustion that had gripped her heart were gone, replaced by something far more profound, an awe-filled gratitude, a sacred reverence that wrapped around her like a mantle.

With her spirit renewed, Euley continued to raise her voice in melodic cry, a holy offering to the Highest God, the Architect of all creation. It wasn't merely sound; it was the language of her soul. Each note poured forth like a river unobstructed, flowing wild, and pure from the deepest parts of her being. Her praise was not performance; it was presence. It was true. It was worship. It was natural.

The wind lifted her song higher and carried it beyond the forest, like incense rising to heaven. The flowers swayed in a gentle rhythm of praise and worship. Above her, the butterflies now responded in joyful, harmonious fluttering. The melodies of crickets and beetles weave into hers, forming a chorus of creation. The earth beneath her hooves felt consecrated, no longer just soil and stone, but sacred ground. In that still and holy space, she stood in quiet communion with her Maker.

The brook beside her glistened in the amber glow of dusk, its surface reflecting not just light, but glory, the undeniable fingerprint of the One who had spared her life. In that moment,

Euley was no longer merely a creature of instinct and survival. She was a living witness to divine mercy, a vessel of praise born from trial, and a beloved thread in the tapestry of God's grand and eternal design.

CHAPTER ELEVEN

Her voice, once silenced by fear, now rose like incense from the altar of her soul. Not polished, not perfect, but pure. Raw. Holy. Her worship was not just in sound, but in posture, in presence, in the sacred stillness of surrender. She praised not because she had escaped the hunter, but because she had encountered the hand of the Deliverer. As she praised, she grew stronger, and her power returned.

And at that moment, she was more than just a deer in the wild; she was a living psalm. A moving altar. She became a testament to the God who sees, who saves, and who responds to those who choose to raise their praise. Opening her mouth, the words flowed:

A Wheel In The Middle Of A Wheel

Ageless God

All In All

Almighty

Amen And Hallelujah

Ancient Of Days

Answer To Prayers

Awesome God

Balm Of Gilead

Battle Axe

Battle Stopper

Beautiful God

Bishop Of My Soul

Bread Of Life

Breaker

Bridge Over Trouble Water

Champion Of Champions

Comforter

Commander-In-Chief Of The Heavenly Host

Compassionate God

Consuming Fire

Convincer

Counsellor

Creator

Defender

Deliver

Emmanuel

Eternal Rock Of Ages

Excellency Baba

Excellent God

Faithful God

Fearful In Praises

Game Changer

Giver Of Life

Glorious In Holiness

Gracious God

Healer

Helper

High And Lofty One

Hope Of Glory

Intercessor

Invincible God

Lamb Of God

Leader Of Leaders

Lilly Of The Valley

Lion Of Judah

Living Water

Lord Of Host

Majesty One

Man Of War

Master Planner

Merciful God

Messiah

Mighty God

Mighty Man Of Valor

Mighty One In Battle

Mind Regulator

Miracle Worker

Never Changing God

Omnipotent

Omnipresent

Omniscient

On Time God

Our Advocate

Our Banner

Our Best Friend

Our Buckler

Our Fortress

Our High Priest

Our Refuge

Peace

Potter

Powerful God

Praiseworthy God

Protector

Provider

Redeemer

Relentless God

Restorer

Rock Of Ages

Rose Of Sharon

Savior

Shield

Silencer

Sleepless God

Smith Of Heaven

Spirit Of Truth

Strong Tower

Sustainer

The Alpha And The Omega

The Beginning And The End

The Bread Of Life

The Everlasting Father

The Faithful And True Abba

The Glory & Lifter Of My Head

The Holy And True

The King Of Israel

The King Of Kings

The Lamb Of God

The Lamb That Was Slain

The Last Adam

The Light In The Darkness

The Lion Of The Tribe Of Judah

The Lord God Almighty

The Lord Of Lords

The Lord Our Righteousness

The Mighty God

The Prince Of Peace

The Resurrection And Life

The Rock

The Savior Of The World

The Shepherd Of Israel

The True God

The Way, The Truth, And Life

The Wonderful Counselor

The Word Of God

Trinity

Trustworthy God

Unchanging Faithful God

Unquenchable Fire

Unquestionable God

Voice Of Hope

Wisdom Of God

Wonderful

Worthy King

You Are A Wonder

You Are My Anchor

****

Adonai – Lord and Master

El Elyon – God Most High

El Kannah – Consuming Fire

El Olam – He is Your Everlasting God

El Shaddai – All Sufficient One

Elohim – God the Creator

Jehovah El Gibor – Mighty God

Jehovah Jireh - Provider

Jehovah Nissi – My Banner

Jehovah Rapha - My Healer

Jehovah Roi - Shepherd

Jehovah Sabbaoth – The Lord of Peace

Jehovah Shalom - Peace

Jehovah Shammah – The Lord is There

Jehovah Tsidquenu – The Lord Our Righteousness

Yahweh – the Self-Existent One

****

The words of adoration flowed to her Creator and warmed her soul deeply. The feeling was remarkably profound. A peace that defied reason settled over her, comforting her, flowing through every fiber of her being. The fear that had once seized her heart had vanished. Instead, there was an overwhelming sense of safety, love, and divine protection.

These words of love and honor to her Creator erected a supernatural force field around her mind, body, and soul. She was no longer merely a hunted creature fleeing death, but she was a new creation, in pursuit of a new life. She was chosen, protected and wrapped in the mercy of her Creator.

CHAPTER TWELVE

The heavy veil of anguish and fear that had shrouded her like a second skin was lifted, carried away by the breath of heaven. What remained was a garment of faith, hope, and love. It cloaked her in the knowledge of belonging, and a quiet awareness that she was not alone… and never had been.

With every whispered note of praise, the weight of the chase and the sorrow of Gayle's death began to unravel, untangling from her soul like mist dissolving in the first light of dawn. The tremors in her body quieted, her heartbeat slowed to a steady rhythm, and the haunting echoes of the hunter faded into the hush of the forest.

Instead of fear, something stronger arose, not loud or boastful, but a quiet, unshakable resolve, the kind that can only be born in the fires of suffering and refined in the presence of the Almighty. It wasn't just endurance that held her upright; it was divine fortitude, infused by grace. Euley was no longer simply a survivor, running from terror and marked by loss. She had crossed a sacred threshold.

She was redeemed, not just spared, but chosen. Made whole, not by her own strength, but by the mercy of the One who walked with her through the valley of the shadow of death. Every trembling step she had taken was carried by unseen hands. Every tear was caught by the Keeper of her soul.

What were once wounds, had now become experiences in her testimony. Her pain, now a platform. Her fear, transformed into faith, the kind of faith that doesn't waver in the storm, but sings through it. The kind of faith that remembers: "The Lord is close to the brokenhearted and saves those who are crushed in spirit"

(Psalm 34:18).

She emerged from the forest not just alive, but awakened. Not just healed, but holy. Her journey was now living proof that trauma doesn't have the final word when grace steps in. The One who saw her in the wilderness didn't just rescue her; He restored her. He rewrote her ending. And as she walked forward, no longer haunted by what was behind her, she carried a truth in her spirit: "The God of all grace, who called me to His eternal glory in Christ, after I have suffered a little while, will Himself restore me and make me strong, firm, and steadfast." (1 Peter 5:10).

The young doe, Euley, had endured a grueling ten-mile pursuit; her body, worn, but her heart overflowing with gratitude. She was alive, miraculously, gloriously alive. It wasn't the first time death had brushed against her. But this time, it had come terrifyingly close, closer than ever before, in a place where she least expected it. And yet, once again, she had a testimony to carry.

The Master had made a way.

Amid the chaos, He had come, faithful and unwavering, to her rescue. He had shielded her, guided her, and breathed strength into her when she had none left. What a merciful, wondrous Savior! Her survival wasn't a chance; it was divine intervention. And her life, now more than ever, was a living declaration of His goodness.

Safe, relieved, renewed, as sunlight poured softly through the canopy above, scattering dappled patterns across the surface of the brook like nature's-stained glass, Euley stepped into the stream again. Standing ankle-deep in the gentle current, she paused, still and pensive. The water flowed around her, as she reflected on the miracle of her escape, the narrow brush with death that now felt like a turning point etched into her soul. Her heart stirred with longing as her thoughts turned to her herd, the family and friends who roamed the same forest paths, whose presence was her comfort and strength.

A deep yearning rose within her, glowing like a beacon in the dusk. She ached to reunite with them, to press her side against theirs, to breathe in the familiar scent of safety and belonging. Euley couldn't wait to find them, not just to return, but to testify. To share the hope of survival, the truth of divine protection, and the joy of still having a story to tell.

With her scent hidden by the cleansing brook and her strength restored, Euley stepped gracefully onto the riverbank. She gave a full-bodied shake, droplets of water scattering like silver in the sunlight. The forest, once cloaked in threat, now felt restored, no longer a place of fear, but a refuge once again. The shadows seemed softer, the breeze warmer, as if the very earth acknowledged her survival.

She turned back for a moment, casting a final glance at the stream that had shielded and renewed her. Then, with her heart lifted and her spirit alight with purpose, Euley leapt forward. Her hooves touched the earth with the grace of freedom, carrying her toward the place where her herd awaited, the comfort of kin, the strength of belonging, and the sacred embrace of home.

CHAPTER THIRTEEN

Confused and disoriented, the hunter trudged away, shaking his head in stunned disbelief. What had seemed like a guaranteed kill, had slipped through his grasp like smoke. The doe, so close, so certain, was gone. Adjusting the strap of his lightweight canvas gun bag, he broke into a slow jog, each step heavy with the weight of disappointment and pride undone.

Outwitted by what he had deemed a mere animal, he turned northward, scratching his head as an unnerving truth settled deep in his gut; this hadn't been just a chase. He hadn't been battling instinct or chance.

He had crossed into a realm ruled by something far greater than his skill, something sacred. And in that silent, humble moment, he realized he had not lost to the deer... he had lost to the divine.

As he replayed the chase in his mind, the hunter couldn't shake the nagging feeling that something had shifted, something unseen. At some point along the way, it was as if the very forces of nature had turned against him. The forest, once familiar and obedient to his command, had become a maze of resistance. Vines clawed at his legs, branches blocked his path and the ground beneath him seemed to sap his strength.

Midway through the pursuit, his rifle bag, no more than eight pounds, had begun to drag on him like a load of stone, each step more grueling than the last. What should have been an easy hunt, had become a battle he couldn't explain. It was more than exhaustion. It was resistance, divine, deliberate and undeniable.

Grumbling beneath his breath, he yanked the bag strap into place with an irritated tug and gave a defeated shrug. The sting of failure gnawed at him, but there was nothing more to do. With a bitter exhale, he muttered, "No venison for tomorrow's feast." His voice was laced with disappointment as he turned and walked away, his stride heavy with resignation.

Rabbit stew it is, he thought grimly. A poor substitute for the tender, savory meat of a young deer, but it would have to do. Still, the taste of loss lingered far longer than the idea of dinner.

His pride lay in shambles, scattered like the broken twigs strewn along the path he walked. A strange mix of confusion and reluctant respect churned within him. He had been outwitted, undeniably and unexpectedly. The doe had vanished, and with her, his sense of dominance.

For now, the hunt is over.

As his dinner had disappeared into the fading light of the forest, the hunter knew he'd have to face an unsettling truth: today, the wilderness had won. The forest, alive and untamed, victorious. Together, deer, divinity, and nature had bested him.

His boots sank deeper with every step, the weight of his pack pressing into his spine like a ghost he couldn't shake. Sweat streaked his brow, but it wasn't the physical strain that wore him down, it was something older, deeper. The forest around him whispered with wind and judgment, as if it, too, saw through the camouflage and into the heart of the man beneath.

He paused for a moment, adjusting the strap on his bag with a grunt, exhaling a growl of frustration that trembled at the edge of something unspoken. Defeat. Not just of the hunt, but of controlling the one thing he had always clung to.

What no was allowed to see was the battlefield that thundered inside him. Long after the gunfire of war had faded, its echo had taken up residence in his bones. Combat had carved something out of him and left a void he had filled with adrenaline, precision, and death. The hunt became a drug. The kill? A counterfeit release.

But today, something was different.

He hadn't missed her. Not really. He had her. She had frozen, vulnerable. Exposed. His rifle had been raised. His aim had been precise. Yet, in that split second, something stopped him. No hesitation. Not mercy. Something bigger, something he didn't understand and didn't dare name.

He clenched his jaw as he trudged away, the vines tugging at his boots like fingers of the fallen, reminding him that no matter how far he ran into the wild, the past always kept pace. He wasn't just walking away from the hunt; he was retreating from a mirror that had shown him the monster he was becoming.

CHAPTER FOURTEEN

The forest had gone quiet, but the silence was not empty. For the hunter, it was heavy, haunted, because the deer's cry still lingered, woven into the air like smoke that refused to fade. It was not the sound of an animal fleeing death; it scraped against the very walls of his soul. It clung to him, rattling inside his chest, demanding to be remembered. It was a sound that had pierced beyond flesh and bone, resting in places he did not even know existed. And now, no matter how far he walked, he could not shake it.

The memory of Euley's cry resonated unrelentingly in his ears, a raw, soul-stirring sound that refused to be silenced. The cry of that animal, in irrefutable distress, had awakened unrecognizable emotions and cognitions within the hunter. Unsettlingly lingering in his chest, like questions he couldn't answer, like a voice, not just heard, but felt.

There was something in that sound, something sacred, almost otherworldly. A plea, perhaps. Or a declaration. Whatever it was, it felt answered... not by the deer's physical skills or by sheer chance, but by something far greater than he understood. And for the first time in a long while, the hunter felt small, his dominance eclipsed by a force he could neither name nor conquer.

With every step, his confusion deepened. He was a man of precision, his hunts executed with methodical intent and rarely undone by chance. Yet today, everything had unraveled. Nothing about this pursuit had gone according to plan. Something had shifted, something unseen, intangible. It wasn't just the wind veering off course or the forest closing in with its tangled vines. No, this felt deeper, as if the very ground beneath him had chosen sides.

His thoughts gnawed at him, unsettling the confidence he wore like armor. Had the forest conspired against him? Had he trespassed into something sacred, something far greater than himself? Was there more to this life, to nature, than what he had perceived? The questions danced in his mind like looming shadows, refusing to be dismissed.

The confusion nestled in his chest; too many questions he could not answer. A voice not just heard, but felt. And in that moment, he wondered if he had trespassed not only against prey, but against Presence. Against the One who heard every cry, who had said long ago, "Call upon Me in the day of trouble; I will deliver you, and you shall glorify Me" (Psalm 50:15). What had begun as a hunt now felt like judgment?

The hunter staggered, his breath catching because the deer's cry had become a judgment, a warning, a revelation. He moved with certainty now, a conviction that chilled him to the bone; he was not alone here. Every step he took felt watched, scrutinized, judged. The truth clawed at his gut: he had trespassed into sacred ground. The forest itself had surveyed him, its existence heavy with the weight of an unseen Presence.

Disappointment pressed down like an iron yoke, stifling the pride he once emitted so easily. His rifle, his gear, his skill, all useless here. For the first time in years, the hunter felt small. Powerless. Outmatched by something he could not name, something far greater than his hunger for conquest.

The brush swallowed him whole, but the weight on his shoulders didn't lift. Every step away from the clearing felt heavier, not lighter. His boots, once quick and purposeful, now dragged burdened by more than his gear. The image of the doe, frozen and glaring at him, clung to his thoughts like thorns.

Something about her eyes had pierced through his usual detachment. Not fear. Not innocence. Something older. Wiser. As if she had seen more than she should have… and survived it.

His breath caught. He slowed, pausing beside a tree splintered by time and weather. A knot tightened in his gut. Then it hit. The memory. It came not with a whisper, but like a scream from the past. Sand. Smoke. Blood in his mouth. His rifle shaking in his grip as the village crumbled beneath the weight of chaos. The child. Her eyes. They had stared at him the same way.

Wide.

Silent.

Accusing.

He had done what he was ordered to do. What training had demanded? What survival required. But survival left scars not just on bodies, but on the soul. His jaw clenched. He dropped to one knee, chest heaving, and forehead damp with sweat. The wind rustled the trees, but not in random gusts. It felt intentional, like a breath exhaled across the canopy.

And that scent again, cedar and rain. Holy. Piercing. He looked around, heart pounding like it did in the desert. But this was different. Not adrenaline. Something deeper. Something divine. **"Take off your sandals, for the place where you are standing is holy ground."** (Exodus 3:5) That verse surfaced uninvited in his mind, etched somewhere in the folds of memory from childhood pews and Sunday mornings long buried under war, trauma, and rage.

He staggered to his feet, unsettled. Not from failure to take the kill. But from the realization that maybe the hunt wasn't about the deer. Maybe it was about him. About the war still raging inside him long after the battlefield had grown silent. About the bloodlust he had baptized as justice. About the tears he'd never let fall. His eyes welled, not from sorrow alone, but from awe. From the sense that he had wandered into a moment not of his making, a space where heaven bent low to interrupt a man on the edge of becoming something he could no longer outrun.

Maybe… just maybe… this was where healing begins. And for the first time in years, the hunter whispered, not a curse, but a prayer. It wasn't elegant or rehearsed. It was raw, broken, barely more than breath. But it was real. A stillness settled over the forest and the air around him felt thick, deified as though he had stumbled not into defeat, but onto sacred ground. For a fleeting moment, the weight of war, death, and vengeance trembled at the edges of release.

But old habits die hard. Even within that holy pause, a flicker of resistance refused to die. A flame of pride smoldered beneath the ashes of regret. His jaw clenched, and his spine straightened as he reached for his knife, not out of need, but memory. The motion was slow, deliberate, and almost ceremonial. He slid it back into its sheath with the same control he'd once used in combat zones where hesitation meant death. "This isn't the end," he told himself, not aloud, but deep within, where defiance still pulsed like a second heartbeat. It wasn't hope that rose in him. It was grit! Stubbornness! A wounded soldier's vow not to surrender, even if the battle was no longer on foreign soil, but within his soul.

His shoulders squared against the shame of failure, and he forced courage into his chest like armor.

Yet his eyes, those eyes, betrayed him. They shimmered, not with tears, but with haunted memory. The ghost of Euley's eyes, wide, wild, and full of something divine, had branded his mind. He had come as the predator, ready to inflict pain. But he left marked, on the precipice of realizing his own need for something more, his own pain.

The hunter had become the hunted, pursued now by truth itself. With deliberate steps toward the cave where his vehicle lay hidden, he carried the memory of the encounter with him, an unfading fragrance, sacred and unshakable, destined to linger for the rest of his days.

There would be other days, other hunts. The forest, vast and untamed, still pulsed with life and possibility. Its rhythm would march on, indifferent to today's outcome. The doe had bested him, for now. His pride lay bruised, his victory stolen, but tomorrow shimmered in his imagination with the promise of redemption.

Yet, even as he turned away, the words of Scripture pressed against the silence: "Many are the plans in a person's heart, but it is the Lord's purpose that prevails." (Proverbs 19:21). The hunter could plot, plan and promise himself triumph, but his footsteps echoed hollow against a truth he could not escape, this ground belonged not to him, but to God.

For Euley, the story bears a different promise. Her body still carried the memory of being hunted. pursuit, The pounding of the heart, rush of fear, but her survival spoke a deeper truth: "The righteous person may have many troubles, but the Lord delivers him from them all." (Psalm 34:19).

Today, deliverance was real. Her cry had been heard. And

while the hunter departed bitter and burdened, Euley turned back toward life. The cool stream had cleansed her, praise her redeemed her and the wild red berries had nourished her hungry belly. As she navigated to reunite with the herd, she carried with her a testimony a quiet, unshakable truth that no bullet, no darkness, no enemy, no past trauma could ever silence.

EPILOGUE: THE ECHO AFTER THE CRY

Unseen but ever-present, a greater power lingered, watchful, patient, divine. The Creator who had once whispered promises of life, not death; of abundance, not fear, now enveloped the woods with His quiet authority. What once appeared as a maze of shadows and peril had been transformed into a sacred gallery, each leaf and limb bearing the imprint of redemption. The forest, once a chamber of fear, had become a cathedral of healing. Every trembling leaf seemed to carry her name. Every stone beneath her bruised hooves bore witness to a battle not just for survival, but for the soul. Euley had not simply fled a hunter; she had faced the grief of Gayle's death, the grip of unspeakable grief, and the paralyzing echo of trauma. And in doing so, she stepped beyond mere survival into something holy, restoration.

When the first shot rang out, it wasn't just the sound of danger; it was the sound of memory, the sound of the past clawing its way back into the present. She had run not only to escape a bullet, but to outrun a nightmare that had once stolen her innocence. And yet, in the pursuit, she found more than survival; she found the stream.

It was at the stream that the trauma began to unravel, not all at once, but like tangled vines slowly loosened by the gentle tug of mercy. The cool water did more than quench her thirst; it washed over the shattered places, carried away the weight of yesterday and whispered to her spirit that she was not alone. She had cried out to the Creator, and the Creator had answered, not with thunder, but with counsel, comfort, presence and peace.

Euley emerged, not unscathed, but undeniably transformed. She would carry the memory of the chase with her always, not as a source of torment, but as a testimony, proof that she had faced death and found deliverance. Her trauma had not been erased, but it had been redeemed. The ache in her heart had become a song, a melody of triumph that nature itself seemed to endorse as she walked.

As she made her way back to her herd, her family, her safe place, Euley knew she was no longer just a doe marked by pain. She was a survivor, victoriously crowned with purpose. A vessel of praise carved by trial. The forest had once threatened to consume her, but now, it testified to her resilience. She had been hunted, but not defeated. Broken, but not abandoned. Wounded, but not destroyed.

And in the hush of twilight, as the trees swayed in quiet reverence and the brook sang its gentle hymn, Euley pressed forward, carrying within her, not the weight of fear, but the light of hope. ***A living testament that trauma may shape our journey, but it does not have to define our ending.***

She was free. She was victorious.

From My Heart to Yours

The message I've shared with you in this book was not just written to inform. It was written to offer you hope and to extend the possibility of spiritual healing as a real, tangible answer to whatever situation you may be facing right now.

I don't speak from theory; I speak from experience. I know healing is possible because I've lived it. There were seasons when death lingered close, when grief pressed so heavily against my chest that I could barely breathe, and the shadow of dying felt nearer than hope. I've stood in the quiet aftermath of loss, when prayers seemed unanswered and faith trembled under the weight of sorrow. Yet it was in those sacred, broken moments, when all strength was gone and every remedy failed, that I encountered the healing grace of God.

And if you're reading this now, carrying your own ache, confusion, or unanswered questions, know this: you are not alone. The same God who met me in the valley of sorrow is present with you, right here, right now. Healing may not come all at once, and the pain may still echo, but grace is moving toward you. Step by step, breath by breath, yield to Him and let Jesus Christ, draw you out of the shadows and into streams of mercy, where your soul can breathe again.

As you reflect on the message of this book, When Trauma Writes the Story, Triumph Wins: FROM SHADOWS OF TRAUMA TO STREAMS OF GRACE, my prayer is that you will open your heart to healing. Not just physical, but emotional and spiritual. I believe that your breakthrough is possible. I believe that the same God who has healed me will also meet you in your place of need. "The Lord is near to the brokenhearted and saves the crushed in spirit." (Psalm 34:18).

REFLECTION

Stories often speak beyond their surface, peeling back layers of meaning that speak to our innermost places. At first glance, Euley's Cry may seem like a simple tale of survival of a deer fleeing for her life. But to stop there is to miss its true power. Look deeper, and you'll find a story that mirrors your own: the trauma that haunts, the grief that lingers, the instinct to either run or fight, and the desperate longing for peace.

The Pain Beneath the Chase

Euley's desperate flight through the forest is more than a depiction of animal instinct; it is a vivid portrayal of trauma's grip on both body and soul. Every trembling step, every labored breath carries the emotional weight of a soul fractured by loss. The death of her friend, Gayle, was not just a moment of grief; it was a soul-splitting rupture. That single traumatic event rewrote the rhythm of her life. What once was safe became threatening. What once was peaceful became dangerous. From that moment forward, Euley ran not just from the hunter, but from the memory of what she had lost.

According to psychiatrist Dr. Bessel van der Kolk, author of ***The Body Keeps the Score***, trauma does not stay confined to memory. It lodges itself in our nervous system, in our muscles, in our breath. "Traumatized people chronically feel unsafe inside their bodies," he writes. Like Euley, many of us are triggered by subtle reminders, sights, sounds, smells that awaken the same terror we once endured. We become alert, tense, ready to flee even when we are no longer in danger. The body remembers, even when the mind tries to forget.

When Pain Turns Predatory

But Euley was not the only one in pain. The hunter, too, bore hidden wounds. Beneath the camouflage and calloused hands was a man shaped by war. A soldier once taught to seek, strike, and survive. What began as duty morphed into obsession? Somewhere along the line, survival turned into bloodlust, and the hunt became a way to feel something again.

What he carried was unspoken but palpable: survivor's guilt, anger, loss, perhaps even shame. Years of trauma had calcified into a need for control and conquest. What he couldn't heal, he tried to dominate. The predator he became was not born from calculated cruelty alone, but from the unprocessed wounds of a battlefield that followed him home.

And so, the forest became more than wilderness; it became a mirror. In Euley's looking glass eyes, he did not just see prey. He saw himself: trembling, cornered, afraid. Her cry pierced something in him he thought was long dead. In that moment, he realized that he, too, was being hunted, not by a creature, but by guilt. By pain. By the unresolved trauma that had made him numb to suffering.

When We Become the Prey or the Predator

This is the brutal truth: unresolved trauma turns us into prey or predator. Some of us, like Euley, live constantly on the run hyperaware, fearful, fatigued by our own survival. Others, like the hunter, harden their hearts, seeking to control or conquer as a way to numb their inner ache. Neither state is whole. Neither state is free. But God offers the traumatized both wholeness and freedom. There comes a moment when we are forced to confront what haunts us, when the chase must end. For both

Euley and the hunter, that moment came at the water's edge.

The Stream of Redemption

The stream is more than a source of water; it is a sacred encounter. In its stillness, Euley found more than relief she found grace. Scripture tells us in Psalm 23:2-3, "He leads me beside still waters. He restores my soul." Euley's trembling body found refuge, but it was her soul that began to heal. In that moment, she drank not only from the brook, but from the presence of the One who made her. She did not earn the right to be healed; she simply came weary and willing.

The hunter, too, stood at the edge of holy ground. In the wake of defeat, a prayer rose in him for the first time in years, not eloquent, not polished, but real. The woods that once echoed with pursuit, now held something sacred, putting a hairline fracture in his armor. For a fleeting moment, the need to conquer faded beneath the whisper of conviction. "The Lord is close to the brokenhearted and saves those who are crushed in spirit" (Psalm 34:18). That truth hovered in the air like incense, lingering even after the hunter walked away.

Only God Heals What Trauma Shatters

Euley's story teaches us that trauma cannot be outrun or erased, but it can be redeemed. Healing does not always come in dramatic rescue, but in sacred moments of stillness, when we dare to let go of our fight and drink from streams of grace.

The journey from pain to peace is not linear. It is messy, holy, and slow. But it begins when we acknowledge our wounds, when we stop hunting or hiding and come honestly before our Creator.

Healing may not remove the scar, but it changes the story the scar tells. So, whether you find yourself identifying with the hunted or the hunter or both, know this:

You are not forgotten. You are not forsaken. There is a stream for you, too. A place of peace where grace flows, fear loosens, and the soul begins again.

"Come to me, all you who are weary and burdened, and I will give you rest." Matthew 11:28

THE IMPACT OF SPIRITUAL HEALING AND PRAYER

You didn't open this book by chance; you were led here by divine purpose. Whatever weight you're carrying, whatever burden presses against your heart, hear this truth: you are not alone, and you are not forgotten.

Trauma has a way of lying to us. It whispers that healing is impossible, that the pain will never ease, that we are too broken to be restored. But take courage, help is nearer than you think. Just as Euley stumbled to the stream, weary and trembling, only to find renewal in its life-giving waters, you too are invited to your own place of healing and rest.

Her story is not just hers; it mirrors what can be yours.

Let her cry remind you to pause, to breathe, to lift your gaze toward the One who sees you. Your Heavenly Father hears your unspoken groans, understands the weight you carry, and longs to mend the pieces of your soul. As Psalm 34:18 declares, "The Lord is close to the brokenhearted and saves those who are crushed in spirit." Step toward Him today. Let His love wash over your wounds like living water, bringing peace to your mind, strength to your body, and hope to your spirit.

He loves you deeply and He longs to meet you right where you are, to lift your burdens, to quench your thirsty soul, and to bring peace to your weary heart. No matter how relentless the struggle, how dry the season, or how heavy the weight you carry, God's love is more than enough.

Today, open your heart to Him. Surrender your pain, your fears, and your sins. Allow Him to wash over you with His mercy and grace. Let Him cleanse your mind, renew your spirit and lead you into freedom. His presence is your refuge, and in Him, you will find true restoration. He's waiting, arms open. Will you come?

Surrender and receive the gift of a transformed heart. God longs to make you new, to reshape your life from the inside out. Through Jesus' sacrifice, freedom from the burdens and brokenness of this life has been made possible.

Accept that freedom today by opening your heart to His love. Come to the stream of His mercy.

> Drink deeply. Let His grace wash over you.

> Be renewed. Be restored. Be made whole.

In the thick of her terror, Euley did something more powerful than running; she prayed. With the hunter's weapon aimed at her heart and the memory of Gayle's lifeless body etched into her soul, she lifted her voice, not in defiance, but in surrender. Her cry was not just a sound; it was a call to the Creator. And heaven answered.

In that sacred moment, something shifted. The forest, once a backdrop of fear, became a sanctuary of divine intervention. The vines that had trapped her released their grip. The bullet meant to end her life missed its mark. And the stream, hidden for miles, suddenly appeared like a ribbon of grace winding through the wilderness.

Euley's prayer marked the turning point in her journey, not because the danger had ended, but because she was no longer facing it alone. Her Creator had stepped into her story. In the stillness of surrender, spiritual healing began. It wasn't immediate or loud; it was steady, profound, and holy. Her trauma, once unbearable, began to loosen its hold as divine peace seeped into the cracks of her soul.

This story reveals that spiritual healing is not a distant concept; it is a present power. It reaches into the deepest wounds and speaks life where silence once echoed. Prayer became Euley's lifeline and her healing came not from escaping the chase, but from trusting the One who could redeem every broken moment.

For anyone carrying the invisible scars of trauma, Euley's story whispers a life-giving truth: there is hope beyond the pain and healing in the presence of the One who hears every cry and never ignores a wounded heart. Spiritual healing may not erase the past, but it has the power to reclaim the soul, to transform brokenness into beauty, and to breathe new strength into weary places.

As you turn the page to the prayers that follow, see them as an invitation, your invitation, to step into that sacred stream of grace. Just as Euley found refuge in living water, these prayers are designed to help you encounter God's presence, release your burdens, and begin walking in the freedom that only He can give.

A PRAYER OF RELEASE

FOR EVERY READER OF SHADOWS OF TRAUMA TO STREAMS OF GRACE

Heavenly Father,

I come before You with a heart that is heavy and worn. I lay at Your feet, the weight of my past, the wounds I've carried, and the fears that clung to me. I confess that I can no longer carry them on my own.

Lord, I release to You the memories that haunt me, the pain, and the trauma that have shaped my days and nights. I give You the broken pieces of my heart, Jesus.

Breathe Your peace into my soul. I don't want to be controlled by fear anymore. Replace my sorrow, my despair, and my weakness with Your strength. Wash me! I choose today to let go of what was and step into the freedom of what can be. Your Word promises, "Cast all your anxiety on Him because He cares for you" (1 Peter 5:7). I trust that You care for me, and I believe that my story will not end in brokenness but in triumph through You.

In Jesus' name, Amen.

A PRAYER OF HEALING

FOR EVERY READER OF SHADOWS OF TRAUMA TO STREAMS OF GRACE

Heavenly Father,

Right Now! I lift up every soul who has opened this book, who has dared to turn its pages and face the echoes of their own story. For every reader who, like Euley, has endured seasons of silent suffering, whose hearts bear the scars of trauma, grief, betrayal, fear, or abandonment, I intercede.

God of compassion, you see them, meet them now, right in the depths of their brokenness. Whether they sit quietly in reflection, or tremble beneath the weight of life's pressures, wrap them in Your everlasting arms. Touch every hidden wound with Your gentle hand. Heal what doctors couldn't see. Let Your love flow over them like the stream in Euley's escape. Wash their minds with peace that silences torment. Renew their bodies with supernatural strength where exhaustion has settled. Restore their spirits with joy and hope where despair has planted roots.

Break every chain of fear.

Dismantle every lie spoken over their life.

Uproot every seed of shame and guilt.

And in its place, plant seeds of courage, purpose, identity, and divine love.

I declare: Freedom is yours. Peace is yours.

Healing is yours.

Not because of anything you've done, but because of who God is, Jehovah Rapha, your Healer.

I pray that this book becomes a doorway, a sacred space where healing begins and new life unfolds.

May you sense the whisper of God calling your name, the way He called Euley.

May you know, without doubt, that your cry has been heard. And you are not alone.

In the mighty and compassionate name of Jesus Christ, our Savior, our Shepherd, and our Healer

Amen.

If you're ready, truly ready to release the weight you've been carrying, to stop running from the shadows of your past, and to embrace the hope of something new, I invite you to pause right here.

Take a deep breath. This is more than just words on a page. This is a sacred invitation. A divine moment awaits, one that could shift the trajectory of your life, bring healing to your soul, and open the door to freedom.

If your heart is open and your spirit is weary, then come, step into the presence of the One who has been waiting for you all along. I invite you now to pray the prayer of FREEDOM and step into a moment that could change your life forever.

A PRAYER FOR FREEDOM FROM TRAUMA

FOR EVERY READER OF SHADOWS OF TRAUMA TO STREAMS OF GRACE

Dear Heavenly Father,

I come before You today with an open heart, hurting, honest, and in need of Your healing. You know everything I've been through. You see the places in my heart that still ache, the memories that still haunt me, and the fear that lingers even when I try to be strong.

Lord, I don't want to carry this pain anymore. I'm tired of running from the past, and I'm weary from pretending I'm okay. Today, I choose to lay it all at Your feet, every wound, every scar, every tear, every trauma.

I invite You into the broken places of my life.

Come into the memories that have been too painful to revisit.

Come into the dark corners of my heart that I've tried to hide.

Come into the silence where I've felt alone and unheard.

I believe that You are Jehovah Rapha, the God who heals.

I believe that You can restore what was lost.

I believe that You can bring peace to the storm within me.

Jesus, I ask You to break the chains of trauma that have held me captive.

Heal my mind from fear.

Heal my body from stress and exhaustion.

Heal my soul from sorrow and despair.

Fill me with Your Spirit.

Renew my thoughts with Your truth.

Where there was pain, let there be peace.

Where there was grief, let there be joy.

Where there was bondage, let there be freedom.

Today, I choose to trust You with my healing.

I receive Your love. I receive Your grace.

I receive Your peace that surpasses all understanding.

Thank You, Lord, for not abandoning me.

Thank You for hearing my cry, for loving me as I am, and for walking with me into wholeness.

In the name of Jesus, my Healer and Redeemer,

Amen.

A PRAYER FOR TRIUMPH FROM TRAUMA

FOR EVERY READER OF SHADOWS OF TRAUMA TO STREAMS OF GRACE

Mighty God,

I stand today not in defeat, but in victory through your power. The chains of trauma have been broken, and the weight of despair has been lifted. By your spirit, I rise, declaring that I am more than a conqueror through Christ who loves me (Romans 8:37).

Lord, let every scar become a testimony of your healing. Let every wound be transformed into a wellspring of wisdom and strength. May my story shine as proof that darkness does not win, because your presence has given me the power to overcome.

Clothe me with boldness to walk in freedom. Crown me with the joy of salvation. Fill my voice with praise that silences fear and proclaims your goodness. I stand triumphant not by my strength, but by yours. I live not by fear, but by faith. And I rejoice, for you have turned my mourning into dancing, my sorrow into song (Psalm 30:11). Thank you, lord, for the victory that is already mine in Jesus Christ. Amen.

****

As you finish these prayers, know that you do not walk away empty-handed. The same God who heard Euley's cry in the wilderness hears yours today. He has promised never to leave you nor forsake you (Deuteronomy 31:6), and his word will not return void (Isaiah 55:11).

Healing may be a journey, but every step you take is watched over by a loving father who delights in your freedom. Carry this truth with you: you are not defined by your trauma; you are defined by the one who redeems it.

Stand tall, breathe deeply, and move forward in faith.

Triumph is not just possible; it is your inheritance.

www.ingramcontent.com/pod-product-compliance
Lightning Source LLC
Chambersburg PA
CBHW070311100426
42743CB00011B/2438